# TREASURE HUNTING:
## STREET & SIDEWALK TEAR OUTS

**KENNY BRIGGS**

Copyright © 2020 Kenny Briggs

First Edition

All rights reserved.

ISBN: 0-692-97469-5
ISBN-13: 978-0-692-97469-8

Warning: This volume is intended for the private, individual use by readers only. No portion of this publication may be reproduced or transmitted in any form or by any means, mechanical, including; photocopy, recording, or any information storage and retrieval system not known or yet to be invented , without explicit, written permission from the author, Kenneth W Briggs or my representative Chippewa Falls, WI. 54729.

Any violation or infringement of the copyright law will be pursed to the fullest extent of the law.

Published in the USA by Kenneth W Briggs Chippewa Falls, WI.

Cover images and all interior images provided by the author.

Background image courtesy Pixabay, 7/22/2017. Taken from https://pixabay.com/users/470906-470906/

# TABLE OF CONTENTS

| | |
|---|---|
| Dedication | i |
| Safety | 3 |
| History Of The Area | 7 |
| Starting The Hunt | 13 |
| Detectors, Coils, Programs & Settings | 17 |
| Display Your Finds | 23 |
| After The Hunt | 27 |
| Documentation In The 21$^{st}$ Century | 31 |
| Conclusion | 35 |
| Acknowledgements | 37 |
| Code Of Ethics | 39 |
| Digger's Hotline | 41 |
| Wisconsin State Statute 182.0175 | 47 |
| Flag Codes | 57 |
| About The Author | 59 |
| Pictures, Pictures, Pictures | 61 |

# DEDICATION

I would like to thank my wife, Janell and children, Jeremy, Amy, Adam, and Tim for putting up with me and this crazy but fantastic hobby of mine. All hours of the day and night working the road and sidewalk tear ups when the construction people are not working at the construction site. Searching for that elusive coin, token, relic, bottle, and many other things that were left in the dirt from years gone by.

(That's me sitting in front in the grey polo and hat)

(our latest family addition)

I would also like to thank my hunting partners, Mike Schoonover and Marty Fankhauser for swinging a coil for many hours in these construction zones with me. I met Mike when we both worked for Chippewa County Mike was a supervisor in the Forest and Parks and I was a deputy sheriff. I met Marty when I started Three Seasons Treasure Hunters Club, LLC in Chippewa Falls. Thanks for the camaraderie.

Mike                    Marty

# SAFETY

**Hat or Head Cover**

When you're out digging you have to think of safety at all times. One of the things you have to protect is your head. Wear a hat of some sort and some people have a cover for the back of their neck to protect from the UV light that the sun puts out.

**Water or Powerade**

Another thing is to always carry water along on your adventures. I carry a small Thermos that hooks right to my belt that has ice and kool aid that I drink. Another good drink is Powerade to replace the electrolytes that your body burns off.

**Medication/Medic Alert ID**

If you have allergies, make sure you bring your medication such as for a bee sting. Some people carry the epinephrine pen and others carry the syringe and vial.

## Eye Protection

It is a good thing to wear eye protection because when your digging, dirt can fly up in your face. You don't know what is in the dirt for hazardous materials.

## Face Mask

I have lung problems so it is a good thing to wear a mask. Remember, you want to be around for many more years to treasure hunt with your friends.

## Sun Screen

In the spring and summer it gets hot with the sun so make sure you bring some sun screen for your neck, face, and arms. It is not a good idea to hunt in shorts in a construction zone due to the many hazards that might be present.

## Knee Pads, Good Shoes, Tetanus Shot

I understand it is hot and muggy but always wear a good pair of shoes or boots because of the rusted metal, nails, and broken glass. Make sure your tetanus shots are up to date.

## Fluids You Come Across

When we are out hunting, we always keep an eye out for possible problems. With the drug problems in this country today, always beware of containers that may have had chemicals/drugs in them. This may include plastic soda/water bottles. If you come across something that look suspicious, contact your local authorities to have it checked out. DO NOT TOUCH IT, IT COULD KILL YOU!

# HISTORY OF THE AREA

**Designs of House**

When you are checking out the history of the area, pay attention to the design of the old homes. The older homes have very distinctive trim outside on the eaves and porch area of the house. The design of the windows can also be an indicator of the age of the house. A lot of old houses have the colored glass on the top or around the sides of the windows. Some old houses have the wrought iron fences around the perimeter of their property. When doing research for the area at the local library, check to see if the houses are listed in the history books, such as our house is. Ask the home owners about the history of their homes.

**Makeup of Sidewalks, Curbs, Gutters**

The next thing to look at is the concrete makeup of the sidewalks. Years ago there was no machines to make sidewalks, curbs, and gutters. The concrete was hand mixed with concrete mix and sand.

The concrete was put on the black dirt as you can see in the picture shown below. If you notice there is no base course on the black dirt so the treasures will be just under the concrete in the black dirt.

Concrete was put in by make shift forms made of wood. Concrete today is put down by machines and put inside steel forms. This was taken in front of my house in 2009.

Our house is listed in the history books at the local library dating back to the 1800's. Also I still run across cobblestone sidewalks and streets. These areas are very old and should turn up a lot of good treasures like the picture shown on the next page.

This key dates back to the 1700's and was found in front of our home in 2009, when our street was dug up.

## Different Designs and Makeup of Catch Basin

The catch basins were made differently from years ago to now. They were made in a different design than what is made today. Years ago they were made of the old brick and cobblestone as shown in the picture below.

Today they are enclosed in a concrete tank enforced by rebar.

## STARTING THE HUNT

Never, never, never hunt when the construction company is working. Always hunt after the workers have gone home for the evening. If it is the fall time of the year, the company may be working later to get the roads and sidewalks done before snow flies. During this time, make contact with the job foreman and see if it would be ok to hunt. They will normally tell you if and where you're able to hunt. If you get in their way, you are going to get yelled at and asked to leave. If this kind of activity continues, the construction companies will put a stop to digging and ruin it for other people enjoying this great hobby.

You will have landowners come out and tell you to get off their property. Please do not get into an argument with them, wait until the construction company digs up the area. The sidewalk and boulevard is classified as the roadway right of way. This is where all your cables and pipes run from the road to the homes in the area.

I put the Wisconsin State Statute and the Diggers Hotline information at the end of this book because there is so much information of the do's and don'ts, the fines and other information. Each state has their own Statute like Wisconsin has. Please read this information so you know the rules in your state. I urge you to search your own respective state for your state Statute.

In Wisconsin, by law, the width of a road is presumed to be 66 feet, unless there is evidence to the contrary. It does not matter how the road came into being. In fact, although this is often misunderstood by landowners and sometimes by municipal officials, the historical "ownership" of the underlying land is quite often irrelevant to most road matters. The state, counties and local municipalities have all the normal rights and obligations with respect to roads whether they own the land, or whether they have some kind of granted easement, or whether there is no record at all of how the road was established. As long as the road has existed and been maintained by the municipality, generally for ten years or more, then the public right of way exists, no matter who thinks they "own" the underlying land.

In all my years of digging roads and sidewalks, I have been in this position a lot of times. People have called law enforcement but were quickly advised that sidewalk and boulevards are within the roadway right of way. In some instances I have even given the land owner the State Statute Number being a retired law enforcement officer in Wisconsin. I have investigated 100's of crashes and had a knowledge of the governmental boundaries for the roadway right of ways.

Be aware of the laws in each respective county, city, or village. Some of these have county, city, or village ordinances to stop detecting. This is up to each respective detectorist to check the local laws where you are planning to hunt. Marathon and St Croix are two counties that do not allow hunting on county property. The cities of Ladysmith, Thorp and Stanley have laws that prohibit detecting. Ignorance is no

## TREASURE HUNTING

excuse for the laws. KNOW YOUR LAWS BEFORE YOU HUNT!!!!!!

COVER ALL YOUR HOLES, I DON'T CARE IF YOU ARE IN A CONSTRUCTION ZONE OR NOT. ABIDE BY THE TREASURE HUNTERS CODE OF ETHICS IF YOU WANT TO CONTINUE WITH THIS HOBBY.

When you are hunting, always remember, do not just swing your Coil one way. When you do an area go the opposite direction from what you searched the first time. From East to West the first time and then North and South. Sometimes you will miss a target going one way but will pick it up going the opposite direction. Remember to go slow. Below you can see the flags going east and west and then north and south.

# DETECTORS, COILS, PROGRAMS AND SETTINGS

When I started detecting 52 years ago, we never had the type of detectors they make today. I used the following detectors:

| | |
|---|---|
| TR Discriminator | 6.592 KHz |
| 5000D | 6.592 KHz |
| 6000d Series 2 | 6.592 KHz |
| Eagle II SL 90 | 6.59 KHz multi tone 412 - 1648 Hz |
| DFX | 3 KHz and 15 KHz |
| V3i | 2.5 KHz, 7.5 KHz, and 22.5 KHz |
| MX5 | 14 KHz |
| MX Sport | 13.9 KHz |
| TRX Pin Pointer | 12 KHz |

Machines have changed in design and frequencies but detecting has not changed. There is a coil, control box, and head phones. When I started, we never had a pin pointer.

My old machine I started to hunt with back in the day is below.

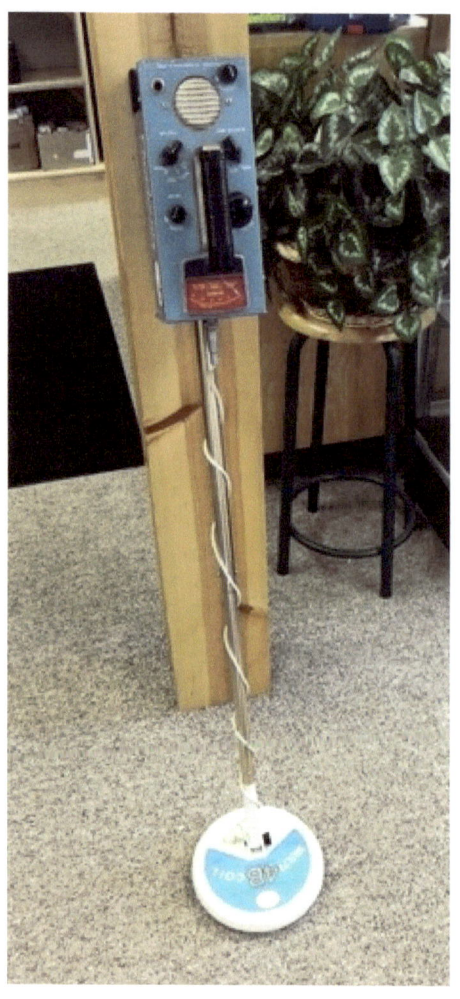

We just took a handful of dirt and run it across the coil but remembering not to wear any rings on your hands. There was no screens to tell you what you had in the ground. Us old timers learned by tones. Not too many people today can do that. That was a skill in itself. We found more of the larger coins lost and passed over the smaller stuff. That is why more of the smaller coins are being found in the 21st Century. Now there are color screens, analyzing screens to tell you what is in the ground and gives you an idea what you are going to possibly dig before you even dig. Some machines don't have a color screens. These days I use my V3i (see picture below) as my main go to machine, followed by my DFX. If it rains, I switch to my MX Sport. I have used other brands of detectors but always come back to my Whites Equipment. You will notice the 5.3 DD Eclipse Coil.

I use the smaller coils first when I'm hunting road and sidewalk tear ups. 90% of the time I use my 5.3 Eclipse Coil. I then switch to my 950 or 6x10 DD and then my 13" Detect Coil. I'm not going to miss a lot when I use this coil system. The smaller coil finds the coins closer to the surface and as I use the deeper coils, I will pick up the deeper coins and relics. I switch to my 4x6DD Shooter Coil when I need a small coil to get under the grassy area that was left when the curb and gutter were removed. Turn your coil upside down (see image on next page) so the bottom is facing up and get under these grassy areas. I was able to find the smaller jewelry and some awesome coins that were missed by other detectorists.

When I hit the boulevards I use my 5.3 Eclipse and then I go back over the area with the stock 950 Coil or the new 13 inch Detect Coil to go deeper before the construction companies come in and start digging out the boulevards to replace water, sewer, cable, telephone, and other cables and pipes. The picture on the next page is the coils I have used over the years in street and sidewalk tear ups.

Back in the old days we never had programs to choose from. We had one frequency and one tone. In the 90's machines started to come out with screens to tell you what was possibly in the ground and how far down your target was located. Now they have machines with color screens and multiple frequencies to give you an idea if your target is possibly jewelry, coins, or junk. Machines today have icons to tell you what your target may be. I use Coin and Jewelry or the Coin Program 90% of the time. Once in a while I will switch to the Relic Program because of the depth. The Relic Program does not discriminate out as much as the Coin or Coin and Jewelry Program. I also change my sensitivity, discrimination, and Pre Amp Gain. It always depends on the soil concentration that you are hunting in. Soils are different in different areas or states. Always remember to ground balance your machines when you change areas.

Mono Coils are found in Pulse induction machines that are used for hunting in the water. They are not normally used in everyday hunting in the dirt. Very Low Frequency Coils (VLF Coils) are the normal coils used.

# DISPLAY YOUR FINDS

There are several ways to display your finds. There are Riker Boxes. Riker Boxes come in different sizes.

Digital displays via Power Point Presentation, pictures displayed on Facebook pages, pictures on your own web site. The sky is the limit if you are truly passionate about this great hobby. A chance to show children who have never seen some of the coins and relics that are pulled out of the ground.

I have displayed my finds at our local Northern Wisconsin State Fair, Chippewa Valley Museum 4th of July Family Fun Fair, Garden Club, History Days at our local Middle School. I have done detecting presentations at our local Rutledge Home for the elderly, the Optimus Club just to name a couple.

My wife bought me some display cases at the local internet auction site. I display my finds in these display cases at the two businesses we run: Chippewa Valley Lock & Key, LLC and Ground View Metal Detector Sales & Rental. These are two of the businesses that I run with my wife, youngest son and three other employees. Our web sites for these businesses have photos for people to look at. They are chippewavalleylockandkey.org and groundviewmetaldetectors.biz.

I change out my displays throughout the year so the displays don't become stagnate. I obtained an antique corner cabinet which I put my finds in, so think outside the box when you are looking to display your finds. Be passionate about this great hobby. This is not a hobby to be secretive about like some people I know. They get hung up on me, me, me, me and forget about other people enjoying this great hobby. This is a family hobby to teach everybody what the passion is. This is not a hobby to get greedy about, so be passionate when showing your finds and talking about treasure hunting.

Some detectorist are good at woodworking and build their own display cases like my hunting partner, Mike Schoonover. Mike displays his finds with the cases he builds in his woodworking shop. Keep an eye out at thrift/garage sales. You can find some good buys of display cases and even furniture like curio cabinets or other glass displays. Some need minor work and even the addition of LED lights or some button tuck to make your finds stand out. Some people even make coffee tables and display their finds inside the glass table. Use your imagination and the sky is the limit.

# AFTER THE HUNT

After I get done hunting for the day or night, if I have time I organize my finds for coins, jewelry, relics, glass objects like bottles, marbles, plates, etc. I make a list of the years of the coins I have found during my dig. You can can make a list and keep track of all your finds from each street, or you can put them in display cases. Whatever works for you. The object is have fun finding items of years gone by. Take pictures and/or video of your hunts. You will never get another chance when the blacktop and concrete gets put down.

**Research, Research, Research**

After you organize all your finds then comes the fun of finding out where a particular item came from and the history behind it. There are a lot of places you can find information from. The local library, the Internet, talking to old people. You'd be surprised the information you can obtain. Your local Historical Society will have tons of information from years gone by. Talk to the local owners of the houses in the area. They have a wealth of information on their home. This is the fun part of the whole hunt, finding out about items that you have found in these street and sidewalk tear ups. There are plenty of books by several known authors, one is my friend Dick Stout who has authored several books about detecting. There are several magazines like American Digger, Western and Eastern Treasures and others that have a wealth of information. A big one is talk to veteran treasure hunters we are a catalog of information. While you are out traveling around, keep your eyes out for road tear outs in your area. All spring and summer, watch for the orange cones and Digger's Hotline flags up and down boulevards. Check with local Street Superintendent or Village Street Supervisor.

## Cleaning Your Coins

Be careful when you are starting to clean your coins. Some coins are valuable and if you clean them, you will loose value. I study the Whitman's Red Book to learn about the particular coin. This book is a vast of knowledge to the coin collector. Years minted, amount minded, mint mark (where it was minted), any error coins. If you come across an error coin, some are more valuable than others. Do your homework and a lot of reading. DO NOT RUB OLD SILVER COINS you find. Wash them under the tap water when you get home. A trick that I do is get a larger medicine container, take all the labels off. Fill the container partially full of water and add Dawn dish soap. The good coins I place in this container. While I'm hunting, the coins are getting somewhat clean while I continue to hunt. When I get home, the coins are not that hard to clean. The clad coins are run through my rock tumbler to be cleaned and then taken to the bank.

## Keeping Track Of How Much You Found

If you just bought a Detector, this is a good way to keep track of how much you found. Deduct the amount from the amount of the machine. When you find enough to pay off what you paid for the machine, then the rest will be clear money. You can start saving to buy extra things or even a higher end machine. This is the only hobby that pays for itself.

# DOCUMENTATION IN THE 21ˢᵀ CENTURY

Years ago I took pictures with my Kodak Hawkeye Instamatic II 126 Camera that I got by sending in Old Dutch Potato Chip Box Tops. When I saved up enough, I sent them in and got my first camera. It didn't take as nice of pictures like the cameras now. It got us by when we needed to take pictures. The problem with this is the film had to be sent in to get developed. If the picture didn't turn out, you lost that picture of your find.

I then graduated to my 35 mm Polaroid cameras to keep track of my finds. Now there is sophisticated audio video equipment. I have the Canon Vixia HF R30 camcorder, see fig () and the Canon D30 waterproof digital camera that can take HD still photographs as well as HD videos of my hunts. I also own the wireless WM-V1 microphones for my Canon equipment that records clear audio up to 75 feet away from my camcorder.

I also have Apple iPhone 6 S Plus, iPads Air 2, iPhone 8 Plus, iPad Pro 2019, 2 tripods, iOgrapher that my iPad attaches to.

I have the Zoom H4n Pro Digital Recorders. I have the Rode Filmmaker Kit Wireless microphone and Rode Wireless Go Microphone systems to record on my iPhone and iPad Air 2.

I also do Podcasts of my finds on my Podcast Show. This information and more will be discussed in a future book that I will be working on. You have to watch what you show to the world because of certain antiquities laws. Be aware of all local, state, federal, and national laws. I have enjoyed taking HD still photos and videos since this high tech equipment came out. I enjoy making treasure hunting videos. I hope that someone will be able to get something out of them. I used to use the Canon Powershot cameras with the retractable lens but after a while dirt gets into the gears and freezes the lens up so it quit moving. My oldest son took photography in college and told me to stay with Canon Cameras because of the great lens they have so I invested in the D30 waterproof camera with no movable lens. Since then I haven't looked back and my pictures are great. My camera and my Canon Camcorder both have macro settings so I can take very close ups of my coins and relics I find. Lately I stepped up my audio video arsenal and bought the iOgrapher from iOgrapher.com. I also bought both the 2x and wide angle lens. This awesome tool holds my iPad Air 2. I can set it on my tripod along with my Rode Filmmaker wireless microphones or my Zoom H4n Pro Digital recorder. For closeup recording and further away, I have my Rode Video Mic ME that plugs into the headphone port of my iPad or iPhone. When I'm outside recording, I always use the wind screens (furry cat) on all my microphone when I'm outside to cut down the wind noise so I end up with a better audio. I can record the audio to my Zoom H4n Pro and synchronize it when I get back home or my shop. There is several video programs like iMovie, Filmic Pro and others. With world of streaming content, there is YouTube, Facebook, Switcher Go, Snapchat and others. I could stream my hunts in the field but that would take away a lot of my hunt time. Better to film your hunts and then upload to any format you wish to do when your getting back home. Remember when your photographing your finds, make sure you have your settings on macro.

When buying photography equipment, don't go for the cheapest stuff because you will regret it later on.

# CONCLUSION

I would like to thank each and everyone who takes the time to read my first ever book. I have enjoyed putting it together. I hope you can get something out of it. I have enjoyed this great hobby for 52 years and enjoy helping new people and especially kids about this great hobby. If you have any questions about metal detecting or machines, please contact me through my web side. Your welcome to sign up for my newsletter that I put out two times a month. I have had the thought of writing a book about what I do in this hobby before I can't anymore. Please drop me a line and let me know what you think of this book, pro or con. We can both learn. Contact me at www.groundviewmetaldetectors.biz. Until the next time, happy hunting and be careful when your hunting.

# KENNY BRIGGS

# ACKNOWLEDGEMENTS

My wife Janell Briggs who helped go over this book and supported me with this project.

Chad from Diggers Hotline for all he information I used in this book.

Mike Schoonover, my hunting partner who spent many long hours in the sand piles at the road tear out.

Marty Fankhauser, my other hunting partner

White's Electronics for making great metal detectors over the years to keep my hunting in the dirt.

And a special thank you to Darren Kirby for the assistance in helping to finish up this book.

# CODE OF ETHICS

In order to protect your hobby it's important to follow the metal detecting code of ethics:

1. Follow all local, state, and federal laws related to metal detecting

2. Respect private property and never metal detect an area without permission

3. Pack out what you pack in, and properly dispose of any trash you find

4. Leave all gates, structures, and personal property as they were before

5. Fill in every hole you dig; leave no trace you were there

6. Never dig in a way that harms vegetation, wildlife, or changes natural features

7. Report any significant historical artifacts to local authorities

8. Be an ambassador for the hobby by being courteous and thoughtful at all times

# DIGGER'S HOTLINE

I know this chapter has a lot of reading to it but was very much needed to put in this book to teach people about the state law and the Digger's Hotline information so in case anything should happen when your out digging. This chapter also has the information about the flagging system used by Digger's Hotline nation wide. I have included the Wisconsin state Statue on digging. All 50 states have their own state laws pertaining to digging.

Anyone digging, or planning on digging, in the State of Wisconsin, no matter how big or small the job, is required by law to contact Digger's Hotline at least three working days before digging.

Digger's Hotline was established in 1976 to increase worker and public safety, prevent damage to underground and overhead facilities, protect the environment and to help ensure continuity of utility and communication services. Wisconsin's one-call center has helped millions of callers obtain information on the location of underground facilities and safe working distances from overhead lines — this is all at no cost to caller.

In the 1960s, natural gas, water, steam, street lighting, and some communications and power lines were all located underground. In 1974, the Wisconsin legislature took steps to ensure that these underground facilities were not damaged. Wisconsin Statute 182.0175 was enacted to require that excavators notify facility owners before digging.

In the mid-1990s, another next big step was taken. On December 21, 1995, Governor Tommy Thompson signed Wisconsin Act 135, which modified sections of the existing Wisconsin State Statue 182.0175. This legislation required all transmission facility owners to be a member of the one-call system. The only exceptions to this legislation are those people that own facilities on property that they either own or lease. This legislation sent Digger's Hotline's membership skyrocketing with municipalities, state agencies, sewer districts, local and long distance telephone, petroleum transmission companies, electric and natural gas providers, cable television and others being required to join the Wisconsin one-call center.

Since then, membership has grown by leaps and bounds, and excavators, both professional and homeowners, call Digger's Hotline hundreds of thousands of times annually. Digger's Hotline has been recognized several times by the Governor of Wisconsin with Digger's Hotline week.

December, 2005, saw another big change to Diggers Hotline, as the company moved to a new location, at 14100 W. National Ave. in New Berlin, WI. The move coincided with a staffing move; the call center is now staffed by Digger's Hotline employees for the first time ever.

## Question-and-Answer With Digger's Hotline

**Question:** What is Digger's Hotline?

**Answer:** They are a free service that you use before you do any kind of digging to make sure you don't damage underground lines.

Let us know at least three working days before you start digging and we will help you avoid costly or dangerous buried lines.

**Question:** Will all lines be marked by Digger's Hotline?

**Answer:** Digger's Hotline coordinates between excavators (such as a homeowner) and the owners of buried lines. It's up to the owners of the lines to mark the locations near your job site with paint and/or flags. Private lines, such as an electric line to a detached garage or other out-building or a line from a propane tank that may be on your property, are considered the responsibility of the landowner. A locating company can be hired to mark private lines.

**Question:** What are the private lines and why don't they get marked by Digger's Hotline.

**Answer:** Private lines are facilities that are owned by homeowners or private businesses and are contained fully on their property.

Because these lines do not cross in to the public right-of-way they are not required to be members of Digger's Hotline and will not be notified of locate requests. Examples of private lines include propane lines, sewer laterals, sprinkler systems, ornamental lighting and electric lines to a barn or garage.

**Question:** Do I still have to call if I'm only using hand tools?

**Answer:** Yes, and it doesn't matter how deep you are digging. State law (Wisconsin Statue 182.0175) requires notifying Digger's Hotline before you excavate, grade, trench, dig, drill, augur, tunnel, scrape, plow cable or pipe. Excavation, according to the law, means anything that moves, removes or displaces earth rock or other material in or on the ground.

**Question:** Why do you ask so many questions?

**Answer:** Many of the questions are required by Wisconsin state law and some questions are required by the underground line owners to help them accurately mark their lines at your job site.

**Question:** What happens when we can't wait the three days and need earlier date and time?

**Answer:** Early start dates must be obtained directly from each facility owner after submitting a locate request. Digger's Hotline can provide you with the list facility owners who will receive your locate request and their phone numbers. All facility owners will need to agree to your earlier start date.

**Question:** How far down are the lines buried?

**Answer:** It depends on the type of buried line, and whether it was installed properly. Although facility owners may follow depth guidelines when installing lines, they have no control over depth variation caused by human interference, weather, or other circumstances. As a result, depths are not provided by utility locators.

**Question:** Why do I have to hand dig within 18 inches of a facility?

**Answer:** Locating is not an exact science, and, therefore, the actual location of the facility could vary from the position of the marks. Also, state law mandates an 18 inch buffer zone on each side of a marked facility. No mechanized equipment can be used within this buffer zone; only hand digging is allowed. Also, you should stay 18 inches away from any utility structure at your job site.

# WISCONSIN STATE STATUTE 182.0175

**Selected Excerpts**

(1) DEFINITIONS. In this section:

(am) "Emergency" means a condition that poses a clear and immediate danger to life or health, or a significant loss of property.

(b) "Excavation" means any operation in which earth, rock or other material in or on the ground is moved, removed or otherwise displaced by means of any tools, equipment or explosives and includes grading, trenching, digging, ditching, drilling, augering, tunneling, scraping, cable or pipe plowing and driving and means any operation by which a structure or mass of material is wrecked, razed, rended, moved or removed.

(bm) "Excavator" means a person who engages in excavation.

(bt) "Local governmental unit" means a political subdivision of this state, a special purpose district in this state, an instrumentality or corporation of such a political subdivision or special purpose district, a combination or subunit of any of the foregoing or an instrumentality of the state and any of the foregoing.

(bu) "Pavement" means asphalt or concrete pavement.

(bv) "Private transmission facilities" means transmission facilities that are owned by a person, other than a governmental unit, and that are located on private property owned or leased by that person and that do not cross a public right-of-way.

(c) "Transmission facilities" includes all pipes, pipelines, wires, cables, ducts, wirelines and associated facilities, whether underground or above ground, regardless of the nature of their transmittance or of their in-service application. The term includes, but is not restricted to, utility facilities, government-owned facilities, facilities transporting hazardous materials, communications and data facilities, drainage and water facilities and sewer systems. The term does not include culverts.

(d) "Working days" means days other than Saturday, Sunday and legal holidays.

(1m) ONE-CALL SYSTEM.

(a) Statewide system. Owners of transmission facilities, other than private transmission facilities, shall establish or designate a nonprofit organization governed by a board of directors as the operator of a one-call system and shall be members of the system. The one-call system shall be a statewide communication system in which a single operational center receives excavation notices and transmits notice information to affected-member transmission facilities owners. Owners of private transmission facilities may be members.

(bm) Membership fees. A member may be assessed an initial start−up fee equal to the system's costs in adding the member to the one−call system, except that any initial start−up fee may not exceed $100 for a member whose transmission facilities serve less than 5,000 customers. For purposes of assessing the initial start−up fee, affiliated transmission facilities owners shall be considered a single member. Under this paragraph, a transmission facilities owner is affiliated with another transmission facilities owner if the transmission facilities owner, directly, or indirectly through one or more intermediaries, controls, is controlled by, or is under common control with, the other transmission facilities owner. Members shall also be assessed a fee per notice of intended excavation activity. Membership in the one−call system ceases if a fee assessed under this paragraph is more than 90 days past due. A transmission facilities owner may be reinstated as a member upon payment of the amount past due.

(c) Liability. Any transmission facilities owner who is required to be a member of the one−call system and has not complied with the membership requirement is liable for all damages to the owner's transmission facilities and for any other damages that occur as a result of a properly noticed excavation to the one−call system.

(d) System functions. The one−call system shall do all of the following:

1. Publicize the availability and use of the one−call system.

2. Provide toll−free communication to the one−call system.

3. Accept notices of intended excavation activity.

4. Accept notices of intended emergency location or emergency excavation activity 24 hours a day.

(4m) Disclose to persons providing notice that the one-call system does not include private transmission facilities as required under par. (e) 1.

5. Inform the person providing notice of the names of affected-member transmission facilities owners who will receive the notice information.
6. Promptly transmit notice information to affected-member transmission facilities owners.
7. Retain records of notices for a period of not less than 6 years.

(e) Information system.

1. The operator of the one-call system shall ensure, through information distributed to the public by phone, Internet, or printed materials, that a person providing notice on intended excavation activity is informed that private transmission facilities are not subject to the one-call system and that the person providing notice is referred to other entities to be contacted by the person for determining the location of private transmission facilities. In providing this information, the operator shall specifically use the term "propane" in describing the type of private transmission facilities that are not subject to the one-call system.

2. The department of commerce may promulgate a rule that requires retail suppliers, as defined in s. 101.16 (1) (d), of propane to inform their customers each year of the obligation of owners of transmission facilities under this section.

(2) EXCAVATOR AND PLANNER RESPONSIBILITIES.
(a) Planning. Every person who is responsible for the preparation of plans and specifications for nonemergency

excavation and every excavator shall do all of the following:

1. Take reasonable action to learn the location of any transmission facilities in and near the area where the excavation is to be conducted.

2. Plan the excavation to avoid to the extent possible interference with transmission facilities in and near the excavation area.

(am) Excavation notice. An excavator shall do all of the following:

1. Provide advance notice not less than 3 working days before the start of nonemergency excavation to the one-call system.

2. In an emergency, take all reasonable precautions to avoid to the extent possible interference with existing transmission facilities in and near the excavation area and notify as promptly as possible the owners of transmission facilities which may be affected by the emergency excavation.

3. Maintain an estimated minimum clearance of 18 inches between a marking for an unexposed underground transmission facility that is marked under sub. (2m) and the cutting edge or point of any power-operated excavating or earth moving equipment except as is necessary at the beginning of the excavation process to penetrate and remove the surface layer of pavement. When the underground transmission facility becomes exposed or if the transmission facility is already exposed, the excavator may reduce the clearance to 2 times the known limit of control of the cutting edge or point of the equipment or 12 inches, whichever is greater.

4. Provide a repeat notice to the one-call system if marks are destroyed or covered by excavation site activities, if the

excavation does not start within 10 days of the scheduled start date or if excavation is interrupted for more than 10 days.

5. Provide support for existing transmission facilities in and near the excavation area that may be reasonably necessary or that is specified by the transmission facility owner for the protection of the facilities, unless protection is required of the owner of the transmission facility under s. 66.0831.

6. Before backfilling, inspect all transmission facilities exposed during excavation to ascertain if the transmission facilities have been or may have been struck, damaged, dislocated or disrupted.

6m. Refrain from backfilling an excavation until an inspection is conducted and any necessary repairs have been made by the owner of the transmission facility.

7. Immediately notify the owner of a transmission facility if an inspection reveals that the transmission facility has been or may have been struck, damaged, dislocated or disrupted.

8. Backfill an excavation as specified by the owner of the existing transmission facilities or in a manner and with materials that may be reasonably necessary for the protection of, and to provide reliable support during backfilling and following backfilling for, existing transmission facilities in and near the excavation area.

(bm) Notice. An excavation notice shall include all of the following information:

1. The name of the person providing notice.

2. The name, address and telephone number of the excavator.

3. The specific location and description of the excavation area, including the county, place, street address, nearest intersecting road, distance and direction from the nearest intersection and marking instructions.

4. A description of the intended excavation activity.

5. The intended starting date of the excavation.

(2m) TRANSMISSION FACILITIES OWNER REQUIREMENTS.

(a) Responsibilities. A transmission facilities owner shall do all of the following:

1. Respond to a planning notice within 10 days after receipt of the notice by conducting field markings, providing records and taking other appropriate response.

2. Respond to an excavation notice within 3 working days by marking the location of transmission facilities and, if applicable, laterals as provided under par. (b) in the area described in the excavation notice.

3. Provide emergency locater service within 24 hours after receiving a request for that service.

(b) Facilities marking. A person owning transmission facilities, upon receipt of an excavation notice, shall mark in a reasonable manner the locations of transmission facilities at the area described in the notice to enable the excavator to locate the transmission facilities without endangering the security of the facilities or the public. Except as provided in par. (bm), if the person is a local governmental unit and if the excavation notice relates to sewer or water facilities owned by the local governmental unit, the local governmental unit shall also mark the locations within the public right−of−way of all laterals connected to the sewer or water facilities at the area described in the notice. The marking of facilities shall be completed within 3 working days after receipt of the notice, or if notice is given more than 10 days before excavation is scheduled to begin, marking shall be completed at least 3 working days before excavation is scheduled to begin. If the approximate location of a transmission facility is marked with paint, flags, stakes or other physical means, the following color coding of lines, cables or conduits shall comply with the uniform color code adopted by the American National Standards Institute:

1. Electric power: red.

2. Gas, oil, steam, petroleum or gaseous materials: yellow.

3. Communications, cable television or alarm or signal systems: orange.

4. Water, irrigation or slurry systems: blue.

5. Sewer or drain systems: green.

6. Temporary survey markings: pink.

7. Proposed excavation: White.

(bm) Local governmental units. A local governmental unit is considered to have satisfied the requirement under par. (b) to mark the locations within the public right-of-way of all laterals connected to sewer or water facilities if the local governmental unit makes available to an excavator, for inspection and making copies, information on the location of such laterals as shown on maps, drawings, diagrams, or other records, that are readily available. If a local governmental unit has no such readily available information regarding such laterals and the local governmental unit provides the excavator with a written notice that the local governmental unit has no such readily available information, the local governmental unit is considered to have satisfied the requirement under par. (b) to mark the locations within the public right-of-way of all laterals connected to the sewer or water facilities.

(br) Private transmission facilities. Paragraphs (a) to (bm) do not apply to owners of private transmission facilities.

(c) Facilities inspection and repair. Every person owning transmission facilities who receives a notice of possible damage shall inspect the facilities for damage within 6 hours after receipt of the notice if there is risk of personal injury or loss of life or within 24 hours after receipt of the notice if there is not a risk of personal injury or loss of life and shall repair any damage found as soon as practicable. Unless the owner of any transmission facility is notified or has knowledge of damage to transmission facilities by an excavator, the owner is not responsible for or required to make an inspection of its transmission facilities, nor shall the owner, in the absence of notification or knowledge, be responsible for supervising in any manner the excavation.

(2r) FACILITIES INSTALLED AFTER DECEMBER 31, 2006. Any person who, after December 31, 2006, installs a nonconductive water or sewer lateral shall also install a locating wire or other equally effective means for marking the location of the lateral. The requirement shall not apply to minor repairs to, or partial replacements of, laterals installed before January 1, 2007.

NOTE: Sub. (2r) was created as 182.0175 (2r) and renumbered by the revisor under s. 13.93 (1) (b).

(3) PENALTIES.

(a) Forfeitures. Any person who willfully and knowingly violates this section may be required to forfeit $2,000 for each offense. Each day of continued violation constitutes a separate offense.

(b) Misdemeanor. Whoever intentionally removes, moves or obliterates a transmission facilities marking placed by the transmission facilities owner may be fined not more than $500 or imprisoned for not more than 30 days or both. This paragraph does not apply to an excavator who removes or obliterates markings during an excavation.

(4) RIGHT OF ACTION. This section shall not affect any right of action or penalty which this state or any person may have.

(5) RIGHT TO INJUNCTION. If any person engages in or is likely to engage in excavation inconsistent with this section and which results or is likely to result in damage to transmission facilities, the person who owns or operates the facilities may seek injunctive relief in the circuit court for the county in which the transmission facilities are located. If the transmission facilities are owned or operated by a public utility as defined in s. 196.01 (5), including a telecommunications carrier, as defined in s. 196.01 (8m), and the public utility does not seek injunctive relief, the attorney general, upon request of the public service commission, shall seek injunctive relief in the circuit court for the county in which the transmission facilities are located.

# FLAG CODES

You will see these flags at every street and Sidewalk tear up. These colors are universal in all 50 states. I put Digger's Hotline information and the Wisconsin State Statue in this book so people have an idea of how complex this very important issue is and that anyone digging know the consequences before they dig and if they should hit any lines while treasure hunting.

The picture of these flags are the same in all 50 states but the wording in each respective State Statue may read a bit different than what the Wisconsin Law says. Each state has a set of statues covering each respective state.

There is different ways and statues in all 50 States to dig at anytime. Some states have Hotline phone numbers and others have state statues to cover Digger's Hotline in each respective state.

In street and sidewalk tear ups, the flags have already been put in place by the local government street and zoning departments.

## KNOW THE COLOR CODE

|  |  |
|---|---|
| **WHITE :** | Proposed Excavation |
| **PINK :** | Temporary Survey Markings |
| **RED :** | Electric Power Lines, Cables, Conduit and Lighting Cables |
| **YELLOW :** | Gas, Oil, Steam, Petroleum or Gaseous Materials |
| **ORANGE :** | Communication, Alarm or Signal Lines, Cables or Conduit |
| **BLUE:** | Potable Water |
| **PURPLE :** | Reclaimed Water, Irrigation and Slurry Lines |
| **GREEN:** | Sewer and Drain Lines |

# ABOUT THE AUTHOR

I have been detecting for 51 years, thanks to my mentor, Alvin Cahoon. Alvin got me interested in detecting at a young age. I watched Alvin search for old coins at the baseball diamonds across the street from my house back in the late 1960's and early 1970's. I was so intrigued with what he was doing that I saved up my paper route money from delivering the local newspaper and bought my own detector.

I bought an old Blue Box Metal Detector called the Discriminator from White's Electronics. My first coin that got me hooked for this wonderful hobby was a 1922 Peace Dollar that I found at the baseball diamond. I continued to detect as I grew up.

I used metal detecting as a stress reliever from my high stress jobs as a law enforcement officer, emergency medical technician and firefighter. If I had a bad day or bad call, I would get home from work, grab my detector and headphones and go detecting to clear my mind.

I spend my down time teaching people who have bought metal detectors from me. I spend my off time detecting road tear ups. I also do presentations and speak to civic groups and organizations. I would like to get more kids involved in this fantastic hobby. If you see me out hunting, don't be afraid to stop and ask questions. I always love to talk metal detecting.

# PICTURES, PICTURES, PICTURES

American Indianhead Penny

1907 Barber Quarter, New Orleans mint

1903 Canadian Penny

American Buffalo Nickel

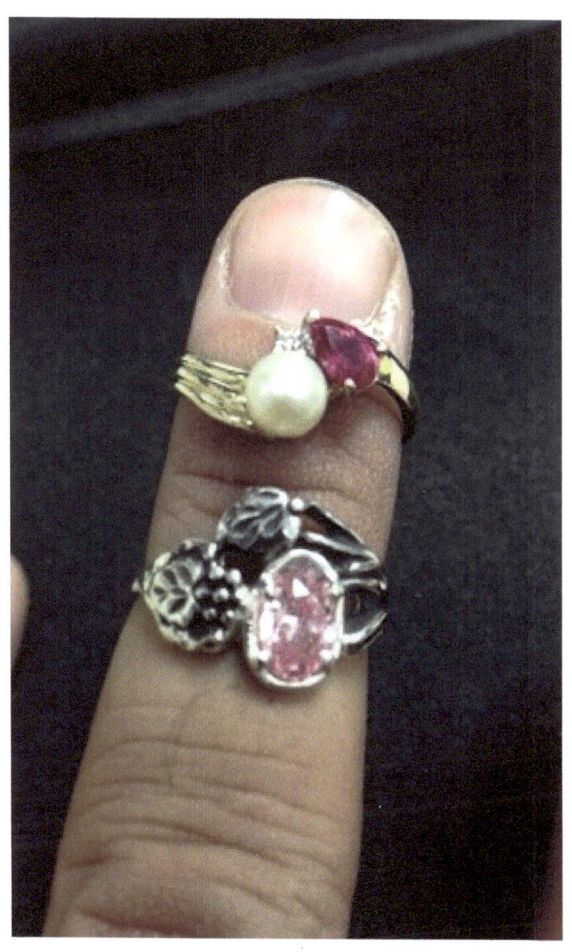

A few of the rings that I've found

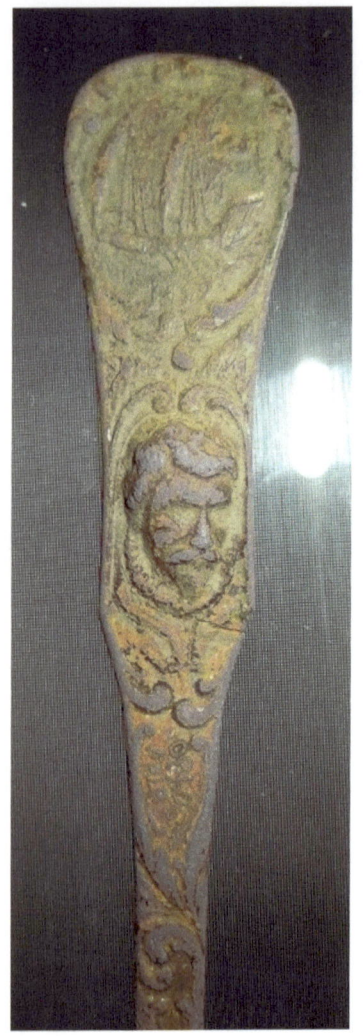

1847 Chicago World Fair Spoon

A few display cases filled with some of my finds

Saint John Vianney medallion

Retailer's token

Fashion Academy Award from 1963

Leinenkugel's Brewery 90th Anniversary medallion (1957)

1893 U.S. Dime

A haul of coinage found metal detecting

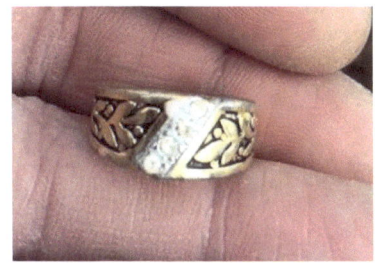

Some other interesting finds

Collection of bottles, coins, locks, rings and more

www.ingramcontent.com/pod-product-compliance
Lightning Source LLC
Chambersburg PA
CBHW042310150426
43198CB00001B/29